C000103934

Longyearbyen Travel Guide

2024

Your Comprehensive Travel Companion.

Joanne Roberts

Map Of Longyearbyen

Table of Contents

Introduction

"Mystical Longyearbyen: A Journey to the Arctic Wonderland".

In the heart of the Arctic, where ice and snow reign supreme, there is one site that captures the mind like no other. Welcome to Longyearbyen, a quiet and enticing destination that encourages courageous guests to go on a life-changing adventure.

Imagine a world where polar bears can roam freely, their majestic presence serving as a constant reminder that this is undiscovered territory. Imagine yourself standing on the edge of a glacier, taking in the majestic frozen work of nature while feeling the coolness in the air on your face. This is Longyearbyen, a place where awe and wonder pervade every step you take and time seems to stand still.

As you turn the pages of this guide, you will enter an entirely new universe. Discover Longyearbyen's intriguing history as a mining town and its current significance as a center for Arctic research. Explore the rich culture of this remote outpost, which is home to a tight-knit community of explorers and adventurers.

However, Longyearbyen is more than just a daring resort; it is also a place of unexpected beauty and calm. Discover bizarre places where the midnight light casts an eerie glow and majestic mountains pierce the sky. Take a boat journey to see the Northern Lights, or go dog sledding across the Arctic tundra.

Where is Longyearbyen?

Longyearbyen, one of the world's most isolated communities, is located in the Arctic Ocean, between the Barents, Greenland, and Norwegian seas.

Longyearbyen, the capital of the Svalbard archipelago, has over a thousand residents and is located on Spitsbergen, the largest island in the Norwegian archipelago. This is the world's northernmost community.

Fun Facts About Longyearbyen

1. The Svalbard Global Seed Vault, located in Longyearbyen, contains plant seeds that have been carefully stored in a shared international gene bank.

2. On March 8, after four months of darkness, Longyearbyen sees its first signs of daylight.

Pregnant women must leave Longyearbyen for the mainland at least two weeks before giving birth because there is no maternity ward.

3. Longyearbyen's only supermarket is Svalbardbutikken, a neighborhood department store.

4. Since 1950, it has been traditional to remove one's shoes in the corridor before entering a facility. This was implemented during the mining era to prevent miners from bringing coal dust indoors. As a result, we recommend taking slippers for your vacation to Svalbard.

5. Anyone venturing outside of town should be equipped for their safety owing to the chance of encountering polar bears.

6. Because Svalbard's topography is permafrost, all structures in Longyearbyen are supported by pillars.

7. The most photographed tourist attractions in Longyearbyen are the well-known polar bear signs and the brightly colored buildings.

8. The law requires you to keep your feline family members at home. Svalbard outlaws cats to protect the region's bird fauna.

9. Longyearbyen has fewer than 2,500 people. Many of these residents also leave Longyearbyen fast. Residents of the hamlet have been there for an average of slightly over six years.

10. The mild Atlantic current that moderates Longyearbyen temperatures leads summer temperatures to average 45°F/7°C and wintertime temperatures to average 9°F (-13°C).

11. There are stories that Santa Claus lives in the remnants of Longyearbyen's Coal Mine 2. People have been known to leave letters to Santa in a nearby mailbox during the holiday season.

If you're leaving town, it's best to take a guided tour or bring adequate clothes in case you come across a polar bear. Leaving the town center without a rifle is strictly discouraged. Locals are frequently seen walking around with legal firearms to deter polar bears.

How To Get From The Airport To Town

Moving from the airport to your lodging is an easy process once you've landed. The journey from the airport to Longyearbyen's main village takes no more than 15 minutes, and you can take a taxi or a shuttle bus. It is not advisable to walk from the airport since you may encounter a polar bear.

At NOK 75 per adult, the Svalbard Bus Service's shuttle bus is the cheapest option. These distinctive blue buses, which are conveniently located directly outside the airport building, are scheduled to depart once all of an aircraft's luggage has been delivered. They will take you directly to your hotel. The bus driver will ask for your hotel's name, so have it ready.

Taxis are frequently available in front of the airport building and accept credit and debit cards. This excursion will likely cost you NOK 200.

How To Get To Svalbard

Svalbard is served by several airlines. The flight from Oslo typically takes three hours, whereas the flight from Tromsø takes approximately one and a half hours. Each guest must provide a valid passport or national identity card.

Several airlines offer year-round direct flights from Oslo to Longyearbyen. Additionally, more flights are available for booking from March to August, when travel demand is highest.

Some domestic airlines fly to Longyearbyen every week throughout the year; from March to August, there are multiple daily flights.

Best Time To Visit Longyearbyen

There are numerous year-round possibilities to experience nature in Svalbard. The best time to visit Longyearbyen varies tremendously depending on your goals while there, however, July is the warmest month of the year.

A visit during the Polar Summer allows many people to experience everything Longyearbyen has to offer!

Polar Summer (May 30-June 21)

The Midnight Sun can be experienced during the Polar Summer when the sun never sets on your travels. Additionally, several arctic expeditions plan their travels during this season. Spitsbergen offers guests an incredible array of authentic, realistic polar experiences beginning in early April.

September is a terrific month to visit because the days become shorter and the sun sets earlier, boosting your chances of seeing the Northern Lights!

Where To Stay In Longyearbyen

Longyearbyen offers a variety of accommodation alternatives, including hotels, guesthouses, hostels, and even camping for the more courageous tourists. Remember that lodging reservations during the summer months sometimes sell out far in advance. As a result, it is preferable to book your lodging in advance of your vacation rather than waiting until the last minute. Longyearbyen housing is frequently fully booked, especially during events such as the Spitsbergen Marathon in early June.

Hotels

1. Svalbard Hotell: The Vault
From: $115
Address: Vei 507.1 Longyearbyen SJ, 9170, Svalbard & Jan Mayen, Longyearbyen, Svalbard, 9170, Norway
5.9 km from Svalbard Airport, Longyear, approx. 9min(s) by car

This recently opened Longyearbyen boutique hotel caters largely to couples and sharers, drawing inspiration from the Svalbard Global Seed Vault. Despite its basic style, it offers a comfortable and welcoming retreat in the heart of town, near all amenities and the on-site Japanese restaurant NUGA.
Svalbard Hotell - The Vault

Take advantage of recreational amenities such as bicycle rentals or patio sitting to enjoy the scenery. This hotel also offers gift shops/newsstands, a television in a common area, and complimentary wireless internet access.

Quench your thirst in the bar or lounge with your favorite beverage. A free breakfast buffet is served on weekdays from 7:00 AM to 10:00 AM and on weekends from 7:00 AM to 11:00 AM.

Choose one of the 35 guestrooms and make yourself at home. The private shower facilities include free hair dryers and toiletries. Coffee/tea makers and private seating areas are among the amenities; daily housekeeping is also provided.

Features

Skiing, Horse Riding, Hiking, Kayaking

Parking(Free)

Airport Shuttle Service(Additional fee)

Bar, Lobby Bar

Meeting Room(Additional fee)

Luggage Storage

Bicycle Rental

24-Hour Front Desk

Tour/Ticket Service

Languages Spoken at the Front Desk

Free Wi-Fi

2. **Radisson Blu Polar Hotel Spitsbergen**

From: $148

Address: Vei 229-3, 9171, Svalbard & Jan Mayen, Longyearbyen, Svalbard, 9171, Norway

5.9 km from Svalbard Airport, Longyear, approx. 8min(s) by car

The four-star Radisson Blu Polar Hotel Spitsbergen is centrally located in Longyearbyen. just a 5-minute walk from the Svalbard University Centre and the Svalbard Museum. After a day of touring, guests can relax in the hot tub or sauna, admire the stunning views of the Arctic from their rooms, or lounge by the fireplace.

Enjoy leisure amenities such as a Jacuzzi tub or stare out onto a terrace, free wireless internet access, gift shops/newsstands, and concierge services.

The on-site Restaurant Nansen serves fusion food that incorporates Nordic characteristics. In addition, Barentz Gastropub is a relaxed tavernwhere you can enjoy pizza and drinks.

Slippers and hair dryers are available in private bathrooms. Conveniences include electric kettles and blackout drapes/curtains, as well as regular housekeeping.

Features

Hiking

Parking(Free)

Airport Shuttle Service(Additional fee)

Bar,Restaurant

Meeting Room(Additional fee)

Luggage Storage

Languages Spoken at the Front Desk

3. Hotel in Svalbard: Polarferen

Address: Vei 223.2 Longyearbyen SJ, 9170, Svalbard & Jan Mayen, Longyearbyen, Svalbard, 9171, Norway

6.4 km from Svalbard Airport, Longyear, approx. 9min(s) by car

The boutique hotel Polarferen draws inspiration from Norwegian explorer Eivind Astrup's spirit of adventure. With its well-curated library, pleasant and rustic setting, and exceptional service, the hotel provides guests with a unique Arctic experience in a warm and welcoming environment.

Take advantage of the hotel's room service (limited-time offer) or dine at the restaurant. Finish your day with a drink at the bar or lounge. A complimentary continental breakfast is served every weekday from 7:00 a.m. until 10:00 a.m.

During your visit, you can choose from 59 rooms with LCD televisions. You have access to cable television for your entertainment. Private bathrooms with baths or showers typically have hair dryers and spring water spas. Coffee/tea makers are available on request, as are cribs/infant beds and rollaway/extra beds (surcharge).

Features

Skiing, Horse Riding, Hiking

Parking(Free)

Bar, Restaurant

Meeting Room(Additional fee)

Luggage Storage

Wake-up Call

Shuttle Bus Service(Additional fee)

Bicycle RentalFree

Languages Spoken at the Front Desk

RestaurantBar

Room Service

4. Mary-Ann's Polarrigg

From: $95.00

Address: Postboks 17 Longyearbyen SJ, 9170, Svalbard & Jan Mayen, Longyearbyen, Svalbard, 9171, Norway

5.7 km from Svalbard Airport, Longyear, approx. 8min(s) by car

Mary-Ann's Polarrigg, formerly a coal miners' barracks, has been charmingly turned into a lovely hotel. It provides a comfortable and unique stay with its mining-themed interior and practical services such as reading nooks, a bar, an on-site restaurant, and laundry service. It's also an excellent choice for singles, with a variety of twin and single-bed rooms.

When you stay at Mary-Ann's Polarrigg in Longyearbyen, you'll be close to Svalbard Church and the Svalbard University Centre, which are both within a ten-minute walk.

Enjoy a satisfying dinner at Vinterhagen, which welcomes guests from Mary-Ann's Polarrigg. Finish your day with a drink at the bar or lounge. Breakfast is served daily from 7:00 a.m. to 10:00 a.m. as a complimentary buffet.

The lobby has laundry facilities, and complimentary newspapers.

Features

Parking(Free)

Luggage Storage

Wi-Fi in(Free)

Skiing, Horse Riding, Hiking

Bar, Restaurant

Billiards Room

Meeting Room(Additional fee)

Languages Spoken at the Front Desk

5. Funken Lodge

From: $167

Address: Vei 212-4 Longyearbyen, 9171, Svalbard & Jan Mayen, Longyearbyen, Svalbard, 9171, Norway

7.1 km from Svalbard Airport, Longyear, approx. 10min(s) by car

Funken Lodge offers breathtaking views of the surrounding glaciers and Longyearbyen. With lavish decor and more services than other Svalbard hotels—a champagne bar and an opulent gym.

Indulge in international cuisine at Funktionaermessen, a restaurant, or stay in and take advantage of room service (limited availability). Finish your day with a drink at the bar or lounge. Breakfast is served as a complimentary buffet on weekdays from 7:00 a.m. to 10:00 a.m. The hotel features 24-hour front desk service, laundry and dry cleaning facilities, and multilingual staff.

Features

Skiing, Hiking, Fitness Room

Parking(Free)

Airport Shuttle Service(Additional fee)

Bar, Restaurant

Meeting Room(Additional fee)

Luggage Storage

Languages Spoken at the Front Desk

6. Basecamp Hotel

From $248

Address: 6J8P+R9W, Longyearbyen 9170, Svalbard & Jan Mayen, Longyearbyen, Svalbard, 9171, Norway

6.4 km from Svalbard Airport, Longyear, approx. 9min(s) by car

The Basecamp Hotel, ideally located in the center of Longyearbyen, provides a real and rustic experience with reused décor inspired by Arctic trapper's cottages, making it the ideal spot to relax. Despite its small size, the hotel has a large selection of rooms, including singles, twins, triples with bunk beds, family rooms, and two suites.

Features

Hiking

Parking(Free)

Bar, Lobby Bar, Snack Bar

Luggage Storage

Wake-up Call

Front Desk Services

Luggage Storage

Languages Spoken at the Front Desk

Guesthouses, Private and Budget Options

Coal Miners' Cabins – Guesthouse

Coal Miners' Cabins, originally established as miners' barracks in Nybyen, now offers 75 accommodations, including singles and doubles, for a beautiful and modern experience. It's a budget-friendly alternative with free WiFi, a lobby, laundry facilities, and shared restrooms in each hallway.

Quench your thirst in the bar or lounge with your favorite beverage. Breakfast is served daily from 7 a.m. to 10 a.m. as a complimentary buffet.

Prepare your meals in the communal or shared kitchen. Hair dryers and bathrobes can be available in bathrooms.

Features

Parking(Free)

24-Hour Front Desk

Luggage Storage

Airport Pick-up Service(Additional fee)

Airport Shuttle Service(Additional fee)

Wi-Fi (Free)

Skiing, Horse Riding, Hiking

Bar, Restaurant

Smoking Area

6. Gjestehuset 102 Guesthouse

From: $36.00

Address:Guest House 102, Nybyen 9170 Longyearbyen SJ, 9171, Svalbard & Jan Mayen, Longyearbyen, Svalbard, 9171, Norway

8.4 km from Svalbard Airport, Longyear, approx. 12min(s) by car

Technically, Gjestehuset 102, which is also in Nybyen, is a cheap hostel. Along with standard single and twin rooms with shared bathrooms and a kitchenette, it offers mixed 4-person dormitories.

Despite the modest design, all rooms provide WiFi and a breakfast buffet.

A computer station, multilingual staff, and luggage storage are among the amenities.

Features

Parking(Free)

Luggage Storage

Airport Pick-up Service(Additional fee)

Airport Shuttle Service(Free)

Free Wi-Fi

Skiing, Horse Riding, Hiking

Massage Room

Bar

Squash Court

Meeting Room(Additional fee)

Multi-Function Room

Fax/Copying Service(Additional fee)

Languages Spoken at the Front Desk

7. Hagen Pensjonat – Guesthouse

Haugen Pensjonat, located within a ten-minute walk from Longyearbyen's center, is run without a usual greeting. The details of each guest's room are published on a board, and while they can email or call the staff, self-catering is the primary feature. The guesthouse offers a variety of room types, including studio flats with private utilities, doubles, triples, and singles.

8. Svalbard Hotel: lodge – Private

The Svalbard Hotel Lodge offers ten apartments with one or two bedrooms, kitchens, lounges, private bathrooms, and washing machines.

9. Airbnb – Exclusive

Airbnb allows you to reserve a range of Longyearbyen individual rooms, flats, and even cabins.

10. **Rysskyi Dom – Budget**

If you're looking for a straightforward hostel experience, Rysskyi Dom is an excellent choice that won't break the budget. It provides "no frills and terrific value for money," according to the website. This hostel has three separate rooms—a twin room, a four-bedroom, and a mixed dorm—and can accommodate up to 16 visitors. The rooms are self-described as plain, but they provide free WiFi, bed linen, and towels.

11. **Longyearbyen Camping – Budget**

The campsite near the airport is the cheapest option to stay in Longyearbyen. Despite its remote location, it includes convenient amenities such as a communal kitchen and bathroom. Rentable camping equipment is available, and polar bear safety measures such as an electric fence and security dogs are in place.

Pubs, Cafés, and Restaurants in Longyearbyen

1. Rabalder Cafe & Bakeri

US$10

Tel-+47 79 02 23 88

Address:Naeringsbygget, Longyearbyen, Norway

Opening Time

Monday-Saturday:11:00-15:30

Sunday:12:00-16:00

2. Café Huskies

Enjoy cake and coffee at this small café while mingling with the friendly huskies! In addition to baked goods and cold delights, they provide a diverse selection of teas, coffees, and desserts, including gluten- and lactose-free options.

3. Fruene Kaffe Og Vinbar

Tel-+47 79 02 76 40

Address: Sentrum Lompensenteret, Longyearbyen 9171, Norway

Fruene is a small café located in the downtown of Longyearbyen. They are proud to be the world's northernmost chocolatier, specializing in creating their chocolate.

4. Svalbar

Tel-+47 79 02 50 03

Address:Longyearbyen, Longyearbyen 9170, Norway

Opening Time

Monday-Sunday: 16:00-02:00

This restaurant in downtown Longyearbyen is a frequent weekend hangout for the Secret Atlas crew. It serves beer, pizza, burgers, and delicious cocktails in a pleasant and welcoming atmosphere.

5. Karlsberger Pub

Tel-+47 79 02 20 00

Lompen Kjopesenter, Longyearbyen

Karlsberger Pub, usually known as KB, is a well-known, tiny tavern in the heart of Longyearbyen. It was recently voted the "6th coolest bar in the world" owing to its distinct atmosphere and diverse cocktail menu. It has approximately 1000 different sorts of Armagnac, whisky, cognac, gin, and other drinks to satisfy every taste, including Svalbard Bryggeri's locally manufactured beer.

6. Huset Restaurant

US$105

Address:PB 434, Longyearbyen 9171, Norway

Tel-+47 79 02 50 02

Opening Time

Tuesday-Sunday: 18:00-22:00

Huset, the world's northernmost gourmet restaurant, is highly renowned. With a primary emphasis on sourcing products from Svalbard and the Arctic region, its cuisine exemplifies Nordic culinary talents and flavor combinations. They collaborate with hunters and trappers in Farmhamna, Bellsund, and Akseløya to offer Svalbard items such as ptarmigan, bearded seal, and reindeer.

8. Stationen Restaurant

US$22

Tel-+47 79 02 20 20

Address: Lompensenteret, Norway

Opening Time

Monday-Wednesday,Saturday: 16:00-00:00

Thursday-Friday: 16:00-02:00

Stationen has a variety of lunch and dinner options, including a daily special meal that features traditional Norwegian cooking. In addition, they offer a large selection of wine, beer, and cocktails to complement the meal.

9. NUGA Sushi

NUGA, a contemporary eatery, delivers traditional Japanese cuisine with an Arctic twist. The restaurant offers a wide range of cuisine including tempura, gyoza, ramen, and sushi. You guessed it too! The world's northernmost sushi restaurant is known as NUGA.

10. Gruvelageret Restaurant
US$90

Tel-+47 79 02 20 00

Sverdrupbyen, Longyearbyen 9170 Norway

Opening Time

Monday-Sunday: 18:00-23:00

Gruvelageret is currently a unique restaurant that celebrates Longyearbyen's mining past. It is great for guests searching for a relaxing meal after their Arctic experiences because it serves delicious Arctic cuisine in a casual setting.

11. Vinterhagen Restaurant

The Vinterhagen, a floor-heated conservatory filled with native plants and trees, is the greenest spot on Svalbard. Relax and enjoy the breathtaking Arctic scenery of Longyearbyen. This remarkable restaurant, which specializes in Arctic cuisine from Northern Norway and serves delicacies like reindeer and seal, has a bright, cheerful setting.

12. Funktionaermessen Restaurant

The cuisine at Funktionaermessen Restaurant focuses on high-quality ingredients and exceptional service. Enjoy scrumptious cuisine and beverages while taking in the spectacular views of Longyearbyen and its surroundings. The menu offers à la carte selections as well as unique delicacies such as King crab and dry-aged Côte de Boeuf, with flavor combinations influenced by global cuisine. Originally functioning as a dining hall for coal mining executives, the restaurant has grown into a popular local hangout and a pleasant tourism destination.

13. Polarferen Restaurant

US$30

Tel-+47 79 02 50 01

Address: Vei 221, Longyearbyen 9170, Norway

Chef Joshua Wing produces a monthly à la carte menu that elegantly integrates Arctic themes with fresh food, drawing inspiration from Nordic cuisine. Vegan and vegetarian choices are also available. The wine list has been carefully chosen to complement the cuisine, with a focus on supporting small-scale producers.

14. Kroa Restaurant

US$77

Tel-+47 79 02 13 00

Address: 6J8P+R9W, postboks 150, N-9171 Norway

Opening Time

Monday-Sunday: 11:30-02:00

Kroa's warm and inviting atmosphere makes it ideal for special occasions, romantic dinners, or simply catching up with locals for a drink. Their culinary offerings are influenced by the changing seasons, and they seek to provide exceptional dining experiences.

15. Nansen Restaurant

US$26

Tel-+47 79 02 34 50

Address: Vei 500 2 P.O.Box 554, Longyearbyen

Opening Time

Monday-Sunday: 18:00-23:00

Nansen's major purpose is to provide the greatest commodities from the Arctic and Nordic regions. Their meticulously chosen à la carte menu includes excellent cuts of meat served with a selection of sides and sauces. There are vegetarian and seafood choices available. Savor these delicacies while taking in the breathtaking landscape of the fjords and mountains.

Activities In Longyearbyen

For such a small and remote town, Longyearbyen has an incredible variety of activities and experiences to offer. Polar voyages across Spitsbergen leave from the harbor of Longyearbyen; these journeys are scheduled so that passengers can usually spend time in Longyearbyen both before and after their excursion.

1. Take a stroll or ski in the Arctic.
Walking into the Arctic nature and leaving town is one of the joys of a trip to Longyearbyen.

Hiking the Plateau Mountain with a hiking guide will help you avoid polar bear encounters. Hikers are greeted with stunning views of the town and surrounding countryside as the tour departs from Cableway Central.
Traveling outside of the city boundaries allows you to explore your surroundings and interact with the local wildlife, which includes walruses, seals,

reindeer, Arctic foxes, whales, and migrating birds, making Svalbard the Arctic's Wildlife Capital.

2. The Museum for the North Pole Expedition

Visit the North Pole Expedition Museum to learn about the lives, times, and accomplishments of Arctic explorers who left a lasting legacy.

Here you will find a collection of real film footage, letters, photos, newspaper articles, and artifacts that document the extraordinary adventures and bravery of the first explorers to reach the North Pole.

You will be moved by the fervor, energy, and amazement of the explorers who came before you.

Entry Fee: Adults pay NOK 150, children aged 12 and up pay NOK 50, while children under 12 pay no fee.

3. Church of Svalbard

Take some time to see one of the world's northernmost churches, built at Longyearbyen in 1921.

The Svalbard Church was demolished during WWII and rebuilt in 1956 on a hill with a view of the town.

4. Search for arctic bears.

Svalbard is well-known for its polar bear population, which formerly outnumbered humans on the archipelago. Polar bears have been spotted near Longyearbyen, despite their preference for the island's north. Everyone who leaves town for this purpose should do so with proper security.

From May to August, when the ice breaks and ships can travel the freezing waters, is the best time to see polar bears in their natural environment.

There are several opportunities to observe polar bears in and around Longyearbyen in a safe environment, notably on polar tours conducted by wildlife biologists and other experts who know where to find polar bears in the wild. Quark Expeditions' Spitsbergen Photography: Domain of the Polar Bear is one of them. Find as many as you can, whether they're in a museum, on a sign, as artworks, or as year-round graffiti on the sides of town buildings.

5. Brewery Svalbard

At Svalbard Brewery, raise a toast to adventure!

When you visit Svalbard Brewery, you may be able to enjoy a unique beer made locally and inspired by the vast Arctic landscape.

Not only was it difficult to build a brewery in Svalbard due to the ice and cold, but the founders also had to change Norwegian legislation to allow alcohol to be brewed there.

Svalbard was created in 2011, with its first craft beer hitting the shelves in 2015.

Entry Price: NOK 449 for a 1.5-hour trip per person

6. The Museum in Svalbard

The Svalbard Museum, one of the island's four museums, will entice you inside to learn about the interesting history and arctic environment that surrounds you while you visit.

You can learn more about Svalbard's geology, geological formations, wildlife, and plant life, as well as the culture and local history of Longyearbyen, through a variety of in-depth displays and collections.

Costs: NOK 90 for adults; free for children under 18.

7. Go shopping and dine.

In Longyearbyen, there are various duty-free shops where you can buy clothing, trinkets, and outdoor gear.

Furthermore, there are numerous restaurants to satisfy your adventurous palate.

Seize the opportunity to eat reindeer steak at Huset, a fine-dining establishment known for having one of Europe's largest wine cellars.

Reserve a night at Camp Barentz to enjoy a traditional Arctic supper in a cabin inspired by Willem Barentz, the man who discovered Svalbard. Your host will provide a presentation in which you can learn everything you need to know about polar bears while enjoying beverages, supper, and dessert.

Whether it's moose burgers, pastries, stews, or soups, there are plenty of opportunities to sample regional cuisine at numerous restaurants across town. You have plenty of possibilities to try new things.

8. **Visit a coal mine**.

Coal mining has played a significant role in Lonyearbyen's history. There is still one active coal mine that you may come across on your journey, even if you also come across abandoned mines.

You can attend public tours of Coal Mine 3 to learn more about coal mining and the conditions in which miners work.

Enroll on a guided tour to have your own firsthand experience with coal mining inside the mountain. The trip will supply you with the necessary safety gear.

Costs: NOK 850 for adults, NOK 500 for minors aged 12 to 15, and NOK 600 for those aged 67 and over.

9. Ice Caves

Ice tunnels on glaciers in and around Longyearbyen allow access to the world beneath the ice.

Take a tour to see the calm surroundings that only a few people get to view. You'll never forget the stunning sight of azure glaciers, snow crystals, and icicles.

10. The World Seed Bank

Longyearbyen houses the world's food supply safety net, including seeds from all over the world.

Over a million seed samples are held and protected at the Svalbard Global Seed Vault, which is dug into the Svalbard hillside near Longyearbyen airport.

Known as the 'Doomsday Vault,' this structure provides a safe refuge for important seeds in the event of a global disaster.

Although the Vault is closed to the public, you can still take pictures outside and learn more about its global significance at the Svalbard Museum.

11. Experience the Aurora Borealis.

Svalbard is one of the best places on Earth for viewing the Northern Lights.

The Aurora borealis can sometimes be seen in Longyearbyen during the Polar Night.

However, keep in mind that the elusive light show will not be visible if you arrive during the Midnight Sun when the sun never sets.

12. **A snowmobile.**

Svalbard is primarily driven by snowmobiles. In Longyearbyen, snowmobiles are the most prevalent mode of transportation. The community has dedicated snowmobile-only roads. Furthermore, a huge number of snowmobiles will be parked in front of the adjacent university!

A simple day tour over the tundra will allow you to see the glaciers, mountains, and icebergs that are unique to Svalbard.

Alternatively, go on a multi-day snowmobile trip and camp in the woods with knowledgeable instructors who can share their knowledge of the area's vast topography, history, and fauna.

13. **A dog sled.**

A Svalbard husky can help you explore the Arctic landscape quickly. A family-run business in the area with over 100 Alaskan Husky is ready to offer you a variety of trips to visit Longyearbyen.

Visitors can look for the Northern Lights, explore ice tunnels with dogs, or sled through the snow on an Arctic sledding tour.

14. **Satisfy your sugar needs**.

Go to Fruene, the world's northernmost chocolate shop.

For a delicious way to warm up before your next adventure, try the bread, hot cocoa, freshly baked buns, and polar bear chocolates, among other treats inspired by and manufactured in the Arctic.

15. **Take a boat tour or go kayaking.**

Taking to the water is the best way to get a close-up look at Svalbard's breathtaking glaciers.

Getting off into the water provides an excellent opportunity to witness fauna that is not found on land.

Seasonal Activities In Longyearbyen

Longyearbyen makes an excellent starting point for a variety of excursions and day trips. Before your cruise, we recommend spending a few days in the city to participate in a variety of activities. Please contact us if any of the mentioned activities tickle your interest, and we'll put you in touch with our trusted Longyearbyen local partners who will organize the activities of your choice.

1. Summer-only day visits to Pyramiden and Barentsburg

During the summer, regular trips to Pyramiden or Barentsburg provide good opportunities to see wildlife such as whales, polar bears, seals, and a variety of bird species. A tour guide on board will present information about Svalbard's history, glaciers, and animals. Following your arrival, a Russian guide will lead you on a tour of Pyramiden or Barentsburg. Depending on the schedule, the return ride to Longyearbyen may include views of bird cliffs, glaciers, coal mines, and significant historical sites. Two large firms provide these tours on different days of the week.

2. Kayaking: summer only

Longyearbyen, located along the Adventfjorden, is an excellent site to begin a kayaking journey. As you leave Longyearbyen, you will be treated to stunning views of the surrounding mountains. When booking your reservation, you can choose from a range of options, including half-day and nighttime trips. Everything you need is supplied, even extra-warm drysuits.

3. Cycling: during summer

Longyearbyen offers a variety of bicycle experiences, including small-group and private tours. With a fat bike or an electric bike, you may go on full-day adventures or do shorter, gentler rides.

Riding horses—only during the summer.

Take a summer equestrian tour to see the Svalbard wilderness. Riding an Icelandic horse is an exciting way to enjoy the clean Arctic air and stunning landscape of the High Arctic.

4. ATV Safaris: During Summer only

Take an ATV safari through the breathtaking scenery of Svalbard, discovering the valleys and mountains that surround Longyearbyen, a home for arctic foxes and reindeer. The driving leg of this tour is accessible from mid-May to the end of October; participants must have a valid driver's license.

5. Hiking: Summer and winter

There are numerous hiking trails in the Longyearbyen area, ranging in length from a few hours to overnight trips. It's an excellent opportunity to explore nature and see Svalbard's chilly interior. Please keep in mind that, to ensure your safety and protection from polar bears, all hikes must be undertaken with a competent guide.

One of Secret Atlas' favorite hikes is Trollsteinen, or Troll Rock, which offers breathtaking views of the Arctic environment. Before embarking on this walk, you should be in good physical condition and capable of climbing steep inclines on rugged terrain. It's a tough one-day trek that takes about 8 to 10 hours round trip from Longyearbyen.

Plateau Mountain sits at the top of the steep valley where Longyearbyen is located, making the climb simpler. The 3-4 hour round-trip hike is well worth it for the stunning views of Longyearbyen and the Isfjorden from the peak.

6. **Dog Sledding: During the winter and summer**

Dogsledding is an exciting way to explore Longyearbyen's beautiful surroundings. Before embarking on a group adventure with the dogs, you will learn how to harness a husky and be introduced to sled control. Dogsledding is only available when the ground is completely covered in snow, which typically occurs between October and mid-May. During the summer months when there is no snow, you can go on canine-powered wheeled adventures with huskies pulling carts.

7. **Snowmobile outings: restricted to winter**

During the winter, enjoy guided snowmobile tours from Longyearbyen to experience Arctic adventures. There are more choices available, including multi-day safaris and full-day guided excursions. These expeditions allow for swift and unrestricted observation of Svalbard's vast snowy landscapes, glaciers, trapper cottages, and Arctic creatures. There are also shorter trips available for beginners.

Events In Longyearbyen

Despite its remote position, Longyearbyen hosts a diverse range of events throughout the year. Accommodations are limited and tend to fill up months in advance, so if you want to attend these events, make your reservations early.

1. **January: Polar Jazz Festival.**
Throughout the polar night, Longyearbyen organizes its Jazz Festival, which includes music in a variety of indoor venues such as the town's hotels, pubs, and cathedral.

2. **February: Classical Music Festival.**
The Arctic Chamber Music Festival debuted in 2018 and has since become an annual event in Longyearbyen. It hosts classical music concerts in modest venues throughout the town, ranging from an art gallery to an abandoned mine.

3. March: Week of the Sun Festival

A spectacular celebration is an appropriate way to welcome the sun back after months of darkness. This occurs every year during the Sun Festival Week in early March when both locals and tourists join in the festivities. The festival will feature outdoor religious services, art exhibitions, lectures, and performances.

4. June: Spitsbergen Marathon.

It's no surprise that Longyearbyen hosts the world's northernmost marathon. Every June, international runners compete in this one-of-a-kind marathon set against the stunning backdrop of the Arctic.

5. August: Longyearbyen Pride

The first Svalbard Pride Festival was held in 2019 and has since become an annual event in Longyearbyen, emphasizing diversity and inclusion in one of the world's most northern communities. The Pride Parade is the festival's centerpiece, taking place over four days and featuring a range of festivities.

6. **September: Longyearbyen Literary Festival.**

Every September, Longyearbyen hosts the world's northernmost literary festival. There are readings and talks by Scandinavian writers, including one in English.

7. **September: Beer Festival**

To round off the summer, Longyearbyen hosts a beer festival, replete with beer tastings, instructive talks, and a pleasant weekend of scrumptious cuisine and live music throughout the town.

8. **Taste Svalbard, held every October, is a food festival**.

Every October, Longyearbyen hosts the world's northernmost culinary festival, encouraging visitors to sample area cuisine. This festival offers a variety of culinary experiences, including cooking courses, grilling sessions, and special meals cooked by well-known chefs.

9. Ending October: Dark Season Blues Festival.
Every year for the next five months, Longyearbyen holds the world's most northern Blues festival on the eve of the last sunset. Intimate concerts featuring local, national, and international blues performers are hosted in several small venues across Longyearbyen.

Frequently Ask Questions

1. Is it possible to see the Northern Lights from Longyearbyen?

Indeed, Longyearbyen is one of the world's best places to witness this remarkable natural phenomenon. However, keep in mind that the midnight sun means that there is no dusk in Svalbard from mid-April to the end of August, and the Northern Lights may only be seen during the darkest hours of the day.

2. When is the best time to observe Longyearbyen's Northern Lights?

The polar night, which occurs in Longyearbyen from November to February, results in a complete day of darkness. Because of this, winter is the ideal time to see the Northern Lights in Svalbard. Your best chance of viewing them is during polar night, but you can also see them at other times of the year when there isn't continual daylight.

3. What's the average temperature in Longyearbyen?

Longyearbyen experiences significant seasonal temperature fluctuations throughout the year. The cruising season lasts from April to September, and the weather is consistently pleasant. In May, expect an average high of around 0°C and a low of -5°C. The two warmest months are July and August, with an average high of 9°C and a low of 5°C in July. Winter is the coldest month, with average highs of -9°C and lows of -17°C in January and February.

4. When is the midnight sun visible in Longyearbyen?

Longyearbyen sees midnight sun from April 19 to August 23 due to its northern location.

5. Is there a post office in Longyearbyen?

Yes, postcards and packages can be mailed from the Longyearbyen post office. Posten Norge is conveniently located on Main Street, near the grocery store.

6. From where do Expedition Cruises depart?

Every Expedition Cruise departs from the harbor in Longyearbyen. We will send you a chart two weeks before your departure that shows exactly where your adventure vessel will be docked and waiting for you.

Simple Phrases To Guide You In Longyearbyen

hei — hello

god morgen — good morning

god kveld — good evening

god natt — goodnight

Jeg heter — My name is

Hva vil du drikke? — What would you like to drink?

Kan jeg få regningen, takk. — Can I get the bill, please.

Kan jeg få menyen, takk? — Can I have the menu, please?

Kan vi få bestille, takk? — Can we order, please?

Jeg vil gjerne ha en flaske vann. — I would like a bottle of water.

Hva vil du drikke? — What would you like to drink?

Kan jeg få regningen, takk. — Can I get the bill, please.

God morgen. Hva kan jeg hjelpe dere med? — Good morning. How can I help you?

Kan jeg få nøkkelen, takk? — Can I get the key, please?

Jeg vil gjerne ha et enkeltrom. — I would like to have a single room.

Jeg har bestilt et enkeltrom for to netter. — I have reserved a single room for two nights.

Når serveres frokosten? — When is breakfast served?

Conclusion

We are happy that you chose our Longyearbyen tour guide! We hope it has been an enjoyable trip companion for you to the North. To enhance your experience, we've provided helpful tips and hidden treasures, ranging from stunning glaciers to charming species. As you say goodbye to this icy wonderland, remember to travel with an adventurous spirit in the future. Grinning, bon voyage, and thank you for trusting us to be your guide!

Printed in Great Britain
by Amazon